Hardcore Self Help: F**k Anxiety
By Robert Duff, Ph.D.

www.hardcoreselfhelp.com

Disclaimer: **This book is not for everyone.** It contains a very large amount of swearing and some mild adult themes. This book is intended for mature audiences. If you are a parent buying this book for your teen, please review it yourself first and use your parental discretion. If you are not entertained by swearing **do not buy this book.**

This is also a short book. The point is not to give you another giant manual. The point is to get you inspired and armed with knowledge so you can get out there and do this thing. You can read this in one sitting and I encourage you to do so and then occasionally go back and refresh on the pieces that you would like to revisit.

If you have questions about this book, feel free to email or tweet me @duffthepsych.

Note about the Second Edition:

Hey, friends!

I wanted to write a quick little note to introduce you to the second edition of Hardcore Self Help: F**k Anxiety. I decided to write this second edition to correct some mistakes that made their way into the original edition, to add in some new goodies, and to extract some of the more useless bits.

Obviously I wanted HCSH to be popular from the start, but I could never have imagined how well it has done. For that, I must thank every single person who has purchased this book or who has talked about it as a friend. I'd also like to thank Pat Flynn and Chris Hardwick who were gracious enough to give the book a shout out on their podcasts.

This is a special book and the people who gravitate toward this book are special people. I've had the time of my life connecting with you guys on Facebook, on Twitter, or via emails that you have sent. It's clear that my hunch was right. There are normal people out there who are sick of reading psychobabble and want to get information from someone that they can identify with. It's an honor and a privilege to try and fill that role.

If you enjoy this book, please join the amazing legion of fans that have left reviews on Amazon, Audible, and Goodreads. If you find me in real life and tell me that you wrote a review, I promise you a massive high five!

Without further ado, let's get into the book. Enjoy!!

Introduction

Alright, let's be real. Your brain is fucking awesome. There's no debating that. It does some truly amazing things, right? Even the fact that you're sitting here right now thinking about your own brain is cool. Let that sink in for a second... your brain is thinking about itself. That's like... brainception (actually it's called metacognition, but that's a topic for the textbooks). I understand though, that no matter how bad ass your brain is, sometimes it's also kind of a huge douche. Remember that one time you were trying to sleep and you couldn't stop thinking about how you needed to wake up on time to do all of that important stuff you have going on? And every moment you spent worrying was entirely counterproductive because it was keeping you from doing the one thing that would actually help you be more successful the next day... you know - sleep? Yeah, that sucked. What about that time where you were just walking around and all of the sudden your heart skipped a beat and you knew for certain that you were dying and two minutes later you were hyperventilating, sweating your ass off, and completely impervious to reason? That sucked too. Oh and we can't forget all of those times that you did something that was truly remarkable. You should have felt like a god. Seriously, you rock. But no, your douchebrain decided that it was an isolated event completely due to chance and took the opportunity to remind you that you're still a piece of shit... just a lucky one. We'll my friend, you came to the right place.

My name is Robert and I've spent way too much of my life sitting in stuffy classrooms, learning from people that are way too smart for their own good about the brain, emotions, the body, and their asshole ways. I have a doctorate in clinical psychology, but in so many ways I am just a normal dude. In this book, I will help you locate your internal armory. Your hidden cache of sick weapons with pointy ends, sharp blades, live ammo, fire, and all that other good stuff. Whether your spirit weapon is a badass ninja katana or a freakin' rocket launcher, I will help you wield its epic power and slay that little shit named anxiety for good.

Look, I get it. This isn't your typical self-help book. I have nothing against Your Hidden Meaning or 12 Steps to a Better You, but those books aren't for everyone. Honestly if you purchased this book, then chances are you're looking for something different anyways. The ideas behind psychology, therapy, and self-help have been around for a long time. We aren't reinventing the wheel here, just giving it some really shiny new rims. I'm going to be talking to you like a normal person in this book. That means that I'm going to be swearing a lot and making up stupid analogies that will make you think "wtf is this guy smoking?" If you can't handle that, then you have my full permission to bow out now. I won't stop the entire class so everyone can awkwardly watch you walk out the door. However, if you're in (I really hope you are), then buckle up, because this should be fun. The words of the wise bard George Watsky come to mind:

...but if you're blocking me
I will soon defeat you
I will build a bridge above you
or I'll tunnel underneath you
I will eat you and excrete you
and I'll feed you to the flowers

If I need to, I'll go through you
and absorb your fucking powers
I put in hour after hour
Let's be crystal clear
I'm gonna get there if it takes a day or fifty years...

So, my friend. I'm ready if you are. Let's do work.

Ch. 1 WTF is Anxiety Anyways?

Put your imagination hat on, because we are going back to prehistoric times. I don't know if you are a dude, a chick, neither, both, or something in between, but for simplicities sake, let's pretend that you are a cave man. You got yourself a nice little cave with some sick stick figure paintings and a little wifey who can light a mean fire with some twigs and stuff. Well one day you are out in the plains looking for some food or doing whatever the hell you cavemen do all day and you decide to drop back by the crib to rest for a bit. You roll up to the cave and notice some other dude's loin cloth outside. Aw hell no. You peek your head in and see that asshole Grock from down the street about to make your mate reproductively unavailable for 9 months. Are you just gonna take that? No way, man. Evolution's got your back. As soon as you realize what's going on, your brain prompts a neurochemical cascade that kicks your sympathetic nervous system into overdrive... in other words, you Hulk out. Your heart pumps massive amounts of blood to your muscles so you can dash across the room like the Flash, your pupils adapt to make your vision sharp as a hawk and before he knows it, you have that scrawny idiot by the neck. This is an example of the infamous fight or flight response. Super useful for bashing the skulls of would be prehistoric cuckolders or running for your life from that giant bear that thought you were going to steal its cubs. Not so useful when you are in the middle of an exam or taking a crowded elevator up to the 23rd floor of your office building.

A bit of anxiety is helpful and adaptive. It's completely necessary not only for fight and flight situations, but it's also the force that will kick you in the ass and remind you that you need to get your report done before the deadline. Anxiety becomes a problem when it's triggered seemingly out of nowhere, when it causes you extreme discomfort, or when it prevents you from performing successfully in life. Do you have an exam or deadline at work coming up? First date? Anxiety is a totally normal reaction to those things. However, if that anxiety is so crippling that you couldn't even go on the date because it felt like your heart was going to explode out of your chest or you couldn't stop crying long enough to take phone calls at work, then it's probably time to do something about it.

This is the part where I tell you the same boilerplate message that's on my voicemail at work: If this is a psychiatric emergency, please hang up and dial 911. Seriously, though - if it's that bad, please please please get some immediate help. Stay safe, friend. If it's bad enough that's it's really distressing you or interfering with your life to a significant degree, then getting non-emergency professional help might really help you out. I talk more about that later in the "Get Your Head Shrunk" chapter. Feel free to skip ahead to that chapter if that is something that you want to pursue ASAP.

Knowledge is power and you have taken the first step toward arming yourself with some real nuggets of wisdom. Actually, the sheer fact that you have decided to get off your ass (or stay on it) and read this book indicates that you are ready to make a change. You are ready to kick this thing in the balls. You won't feel 100% better this very moment, but I promise you that you are definitely on your way. Just keep swimming.

Okay, enough with the encouragement and introductory stuff. You want to get started with the actual helping part. Me too. Let's do it. In the next chapter I'm going to talk about the nifty ways your douchebrain influences your actions and how that comes back around to bite you in the ass with anxiety.

Ch. 2 The Triforce

One of the most effective forms of therapy for anxiety out there in shrink land is called cognitive behavioral therapy or CBT. CBT has lots of theories and techniques, but the one that I want you to focus on is called the "cognitive triangle". It's super simple... no really it is, check it out:

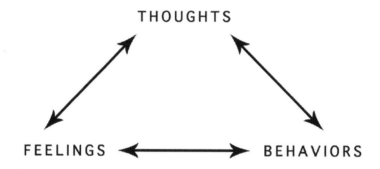

There it is. The triforce of mental douchebaggery. Let's break it down a bit. Basically what the cognitive triangle acknowledges is that your thoughts, feelings and behaviors all influence each other. If I asked you to imagine about someone that you love getting in a terrible car crash, it would probably make you feel pretty terrible. On the contrary, if I asked you to imagine opening your kitchen cabinet and suddenly $1,000,000 falls out, you'd probably feel pretty awesome. That is an example of how thoughts influence your feelings. See? Told you it was simple.

Let's take it a step further. Say you had the deluge of cash fall on your head. Awesome right? Well maybe.

Where did this money come from? With great cash comes great responsibility and now you have a fat stack of money from god knows where. If your thought is that maybe this is drug money hidden in your house by some ultra-violent drug cartel, you probably are not going to be on cloud nine anymore, which will in turn cause you to behave a certain way. You're probably going to freak out and call the cops or something. If instead you remembered that you had entered a giveaway at the mall for $1,000,000, then you are likely going to attribute it to that and instead behave like a raving lunatic and hop around the room hootin' and hollerin'. See what we did there? Your thoughts led to feelings, which then influenced your behavior. It's not a difficult concept in general, but sometimes we don't even know the ways that our thinking is influencing our feelings and behaviors.

Our thoughts might be loosely rooted in reality, but they sure as hell don't always stay there. When you have unhelpful thinking that makes you feel crappy or act in ways that are not in line with your typical self, we refer to these thoughts as maladaptive cognitions or cognitive distortions. It's a fancy way of describing thoughts that sabotage you. Like I said at the start, sometimes your brain is an asshole. There are a lot of different cognitive distortions, so this is certainly not an exhaustive list, but these are some of the most common. I'll be really surprised if you don't find yourself nodding along and saying, "Damn, that's just like me," as you read through these. Don't freak out. Everyone engages in unhelpful thinking sometimes. It's the amount and the effects of that thinking that matter.

Filtering: Some of you out there probably are superhuman at your ability to engage in this one. This is where you take the negative details about a situation and magnify them, while filtering out all of the positive features of the situation.

> *Example:* You go on a date with someone and halfway through dinner, you excuse yourself to the bathroom and realize that you've had a dried up booger hanging out of your nose. Smooth move. For the rest of the night, you somehow feel like you are the biggest idiot ever and completely disgusting because of this natural bodily foible. The fact that you two share a passion for kittens, fed each other flirty bites of decadent dessert, and plan on going another date in the future is completely dwarfed by your dwelling on that stupid freaking booger.

Overgeneralization: You already know this one. This is where we take one event or piece of evidence and jump to a general conclusion. Your brain is a terrible scientist.

> *Example:* You are taking a full load of classes and in the midst of some family drama happening at home, you totally bomb your midterm for that one class that you hate with the instructor that smells like soup. From this point on, you know for certain that you're a bad student because you screwed up on that midterm. Don't worry about the fact that you still have a pretty great GPA and really won't do that bad in the class when all is said and done…

Polarized thinking: This one we can blame daisies for. Remember, "He loves me. He loves me not?" How come we don't say, "He loves me. He's into me. He doesn't like my friends. He wants to be just friends. He doesn't swing that way. He's not sure yet, but he is having a good time at the moment?" You get the point. <u>Not everything is black and white</u>, but when you engage in polarized thinking, there are no such things as shades of grey (not the book...perv).

> *Example:* You group your personal or work projects into successes and failures. If you reached the end goal it was a success, if you didn't it was a failure. Despite the fact that you can gain a lot of insight and skills from the process of pursuing a goal and ultimately not reaching it the first time, you didn't make it and that's all the matters... right?

Catastrophizing: Basically being a drama queen/king. This one makes you overthink and magnify the effects that a situation has on you. Picture the soccer players that flop like theatrical fish when they barely get brushed by an opposing player. Playa, please.

> *Example:* You went to the doctor and found out that, in their opinion, your BMI is higher than it should be based on the charts for your age and height. Surely this means that you are obese and will likely get diabetes, never run that marathon you've dreamed of, and ultimately die alone...

Shoulds: This one can also go by oughts or musterbation, as Albert Ellis coined. Basically, you direct "should statements" at yourself that make you feel really bad. You should be patient, you should be reliable, you should get along well with others... you see where this is going. This is a common thing that people actually think is a good strategy for self-discipline, but it seems to backfire more often than not.

Example: In accordance with your New Year's resolutions, you have told yourself that you should not eat donuts. When you do this, you start to think of yourself as someone who shouldn't eat donuts and further, as someone who is better because they don't eat donuts (damn, I want a donut right now). What happens when you slip, fall and your mouth lands around a delicious donut? You feel like utter garbage, because you told yourself that it was something that you must not do instead of being more realistic and telling yourself that it's something that you want to do, but will try to avoid for the sake of your physical wellbeing. We all know shit happens, and musterbation only compounds the bad feelings that you get after "falling off the wagon."

Mind Reading: Yeah, I'm talking to you. This is one that MANY of us are guilty of. Mind reading is very much what it sounds like. You assume that you know a person's thoughts or internal motives, even though in reality you are just taking guesses.

Example: You text your significant other saying how much you love them and that you are really happy that things have been great lately. You ask them if they want to go to a movie later. I'm talking super cutesy with emojis and everything. Five minutes later, you get the response, "K." That's it, just... K. When you see your partner later you say, "So you don't want to go to the movies?" You're already pissed because you assume that they don't care as much as you given their lackluster response. If they cared as much, they would have used an equivalent number of emojis... duh. In reality, they were just driving on the freeway and cared enough about you to not get killed by texting while driving.

Fortune Telling: This is a close relative of mind reading. The difference is that in fortune telling, you are assuming that you can predict the future and outcome of a given situation. In reality, it's most often impossible to know the outcome of a situation until it has already passed.

> *Example:* Say you are a musician and you have a gig coming up tonight. You may have prepared plenty and your set list is on point, but you have yourself convinced that you are going to bomb and that everyone in that city sucks. I bet you aren't feeling too hot or treating the people around you very nicely. In fact, that might even lead to you blowing it hard at your gig where you otherwise might have killed it. Hmmm... curious indeed.

Personalizing: Personalizing sucks. This is that little trick your brain does where you attribute a personal meaning to things that actually have absolutely nothing to do with you.

> *Example:* Mom comes home. You ask how her day was and you notice a strange inflection in her voice. You assume that it obviously has something to do with you and are left wondering for the rest of the night what the heck you did to make her so annoyed at you. In reality, her boss chewed her out right before she left work about something that was someone else's fault.

Alright. That's about enough of those for now. Like I said before, if you found that you have engaged in a few or even all of those patterns of thinking, you are not alone. We all do. I'm sure you can start to see how engaging in these messed up thoughts a little bit too much could lead you down some stressful roads. There is something you can start doing right now that will help you grab negative thinking by the balls. It's as easy as ABC.

You might be reading this on a Kindle or whatever, but you should probably grab a piece of paper for this next part. Or you can just use your laptop, tablet, etc., which is probably sitting right next to you as well. You technojunkie. I am going to take you through an exercise that is mega simple, but super effective. It's helped a great deal of my clients and friends who have been patient enough to put up with me. It's called an ABC thought log and it basically takes that cognitive triangle and uses it to break down a situation into its component parts, so that you can see where you shooting yourself in the foot. Grasping the concept is simple. Mastering it takes a little practice. Start off by drawing a little grid like this:

A	
B	
C	

Now I want you to think for a bit about a situation recently that made you anxious. Got it? Sweet. So go ahead and put the event that happened up in the A box. I will play along with you here and fill in my own situation in my thought log. So in the A section of the box, I will put that my friend texted me and said that we needed to talk. That's it, just the event that caused the stress in the first place.

Next, you're going to hop down to the C portion because you're a rebel and fuck the alphabet anyways. The C part is for you to write down what you felt in that situation. Try to avoid using thinking words and instead just describe how it made you feel. In my case I felt worried, scared and frantic. You're probably wondering how I hopped from my A all the way to my very dramatic C. Well that is exactly what you should be wondering, because that is what we need to fill into the B section: our thoughts about the situation. In my example, this friend was someone that has some pretty serious health issues and I thought the bastard was trying to die on me.

Let's pull back the curtain a little bit. A = **A**ctivating event, B = **B**eliefs, and C = emotional **C**onsequence. If my friend let me know that we need to talk in a vacuum without any other influences, it would not be a bad thing in and of itself. Unfortunately, that's not how things work and instead, my jerk of a noggin had to interpret the event through the lens of my beliefs about the situation. Since I think that he is calling to tell me that he's dying, I'm sure as hell going to feel pretty crappy.

Take a second to look through the cognitive distortions that I defined a little earlier. Can you see any of them that seem similar to my beliefs in this situation? I'm definitely engaging in a little bit of fortune telling. I don't know what he is going to tell me, but that's not stopping me from emotionally reacting with stress and anxiety. I'm probably doing a little bit of catastrophizing too, since he's really been in pretty good health lately. Do the same thing for your Bs. See if you can identify some of those maladaptive thought patterns. I bet you can. I encourage you to write them down as well next to what you wrote in the B section.

A	Friend texted me saying "we need to talk"
B	Friend is dying (fortune telling, catastrophizing)
C	Anxiety, stress, panic, freakin' out, etc.

The next step in using a thought log like this is to challenge your negative thinking patterns. Pretend like you're a lawyer and your brain is on the stand. You get to ask it questions and hopefully reveal that it is guilty of sabotaging your sanity. How are you sure that he wants to tell you that he's dying? Has he ever wanted to talk about other important things? Did you have something that you are working on together that might have had a snag? Once you develop a few good alternatives to your unhelpful belief, try them on for size.

Scratch out your original B and instead put in an alternative. In my case, I can replace, "I think he's dying," with, "He screwed up on our project and we are back to the drawing board." Does that change anything? Sure it does. Now my C is boiling rage and anger instead of anxiety. Not that much better. Let's try another. Maybe he wanted my advice about a new girl that he is seeing, because he knows that my game is hella tight. That actually makes my C transform into positive things like happiness and pride. Much better.

A	Friend texted me saying "we need to talk"
B	~~Friend is dying~~ Needs advice
C	Happiness, pride, feeling like a Casanova

It is important to evaluate the likelihood of each of your alternate possibilities. Sure, you can plug in the B that you're going to suddenly going to win a zillion dollars, but that's not really going to change your mood too much unless the percentage likelihood of that actually occurring is at least moderately high. The beauty of this process is that much of the time, our beliefs that lead to anxiety (or depression for that matter) are distorted and off base. At the very least, they are hugely magnified versions of the real thing. I encourage you to try this process out with your own ABCs. Be a scientist and develop a few alternative hypotheses. What else could be true about the situation that might not be as upsetting? In other words, how can you replace that bitch of B with something more realistic and less self-sabotaging?

This may seem simple, but trust me when I say that it takes some practice and that when it is used consistently, it's a crazy powerful tool. The trick is repetition. You need to use this technique so many times that it seeps into your bones. When you first start doing this, it serves as more of an intellectual exercise. The brain a nifty organ, but it's also a lazy ass one. It is great at learning new skills, grouping large bits of information, and forging new pathways. Once it's built those synaptic shortcuts, though, it couldn't be bothered to listen to your silly notions of change and progress. This means that you really have to beat it into submission. You need to say, "Hey, asshole. I don't care if you want to or not. We are going to keep thinking this way until you get the hang of it." Once you force feed it knowledge like that consistently over time, you will internalize the process and apply it to your life instantly without even realizing it. Real change can happen using this technique, I promise.

So here's the thing. This technique is effective, but not it's not perfect for everyone. We are all different and for some of us, our anxiety is not cognitively driven (driven by thoughts), but it is somatically (physically) driven. What good is working through the ABCs if you can't even identify any particular activating event? Sometimes your heart and mind seem to start racing for no apparent reason and you are left sitting in the parking lot trying to cool your damn jets before you can even get out of the car. If you are like that, then this next chapter is for you.

Ch. 3 Your Body is an Asshole too

If you thought your mind had a monopoly on screwing you over, you were sorely mistaken. Your body seems to be in cahoots with the boss upstairs and has its very own contributions to that lovely beast we call anxiety. Don't worry if you are one of those lucky people who seem to have anxiety that is primarily driven by physical symptoms. You're not S.O.L. We just need to approach things a little differently.

Physical anxiety symptoms vary from person to person, but there are some that tend to be pretty consistent:

- Pounding heartbeat
- Shakiness
- Shortness of breath or hyperventilation
- Sour stomach
- Headache
- Dizziness
- Feeling of pressure on chest
- Sweating
- Feeling of choking
- Chills or hot flashes

I bet you've felt a few of those suckers before. Maybe you've even had a panic attack, which is basically when you have intense fear plus a few of those symptoms and it pops up all of the sudden and prevents you from functioning normally. Panic attacks and the physical anxiety symptoms in general are scary as hell. I don't get to that point often, but I have been there before and I've seen it occur in others countless times. When you have a panic attack, it feels like you are going to die. You might even webMD yourself (never webMD yourself) and find that your symptom profile is strikingly similar to a heart attack... I bet that realization did wonders for your anxiety. Here's the thing, though. I know it hurts, I know it sucks and it feels like you are going to die, but you will not. People don't die from panic attacks. It just doesn't happen. Your body is a dick, but it's not going to let you self-destruct like that. Even though the emotional pain and physical discomfort may be quite unbearable, anxiety will not physically hurt you.

Great. Now that we've gotten that out in the table, we can pack up and go home right? Problem solved? Probably not. Realizing that you are experiencing symptoms of panic and not having a legitimate medical emergency can help to bring down your stress level a little and it might stop you from needlessly calling the ambulance, but it still sucks really bad. That's okay, there's still more that we can do to help. I'm going to tell you something really important here and I want you to memorize it. *Symptoms of panic are fundamentally incompatible with deep breathing.* Let me say that again. ***Symptoms of panic are fundamentally incompatible with deep breathing.*** Got it? What I'm trying I say is that the process of breathing deeply, focusing your mind on your breath, and taking in a larger amount of oxygen will start to break down those physiological symptoms of anxiety. Imagine that your anxiety symptoms are a raging fire. Deep breathing is like turning on the sprinklers. The fire might continue to smolder, but it's definitely not going to be raging anymore. The last time you were freaking the hell out due to anxiety and you were in the presence of someone else who told you, "Breathe. Just breathe," you probably felt like punching them in the face, right? That's because you suck at breathing. Let me teach you how to suck less.

The reason that you haven't been able to simply breathe your way out of a panic attack is because you haven't effectively practiced breathing. Practice breathing? Yes. Imagine that you are playing basketball. In fact, imagine that you are on an NBA team playing in front of a ginormous crowd. Pretty sweet, right? It is until you get fouled and have to step up to the free throw line and remember that you never practiced free throws during training. Now that the heat is on and you don't have that bionic muscle memory that most professional players have, you sure as hell aren't going to be very consistent in your shots. Breathing is the same way.

I want you to think of breathing as a tool that you have in your tool belt. In order for you to effectively use that tool under pressure (like a panic attack), you need to first practice under non-stressful conditions. Then you keep practicing until it becomes second nature and you can press that big shiny relaxation button at a moment's notice. Once you achieve that level of comfort and mastery with deep breathing, you will have added another awesome weapon to your anxiety slaying armory. While it probably won't solve the root of your anxiety symptoms, it WILL bring you down a couple notches and help you think more clearly. You can also think of it this way. Say you wanted to learn how to shoot a bow and arrow in order to hunt your food. Well the first time you decide to go out and practice, it probably shouldn't be when a lion is chasing you down. You will likely shoot wildly and miss your target. If instead you practice your shooting intentionally over time on other objects, you are much more likely to hit that lion exactly where you want to when they do show up.

What kind of breathing am I talking about? There are approximately one zillion different kinds of breathing exercises out there (seriously, google it). All of the different techniques have their own merits and most of the ones that I have tried are effective. There's no mystic voodoo here. In my opinion, there are basically two main components that make breathing exercises effective. The first one is obvious, they prompt you to take deeper, slower breaths. Basically the exact opposite of what the anxiety monster is telling you to do. The other one is that they trick you into focusing on something other than your sense of impending doom. This sort of breathing is effortful and if you are trying to keep track of *how* you are breathing, it is going to help take your mind off of flipping out. Here's one that is quick and dirty, but works wonders for me.

It's called 4-7-8 breathing. I don't even remember where I learned this one, but it's come to my rescue for many a close call. I hope you can count, because that's all you have to do for this one. Breathe in for 4 counts (you can count faster or slower depending on comfort), hold that breath for 7, and then release for 8. I know I said there's no voodoo involved in these, but for me, these numbers are magic. As soon as I hit my second or third 8 count exhale, I can feel the relaxation inject itself into my bloodstream like I'm mainlining tranquility itself.

The beauty of using this technique to cope with anxiety is that it's not an obvious one. You don't look like some tool sitting cross legged, touching your belly button, and exhaling "ahhhhhhhhh" with every outbreath. You can look like a tool on your own time. When you are in the middle of a coffee shop and you feel the monster creeping up, you don't want to worry about looking like a tool. You can use 4-7-8 without anyone else knowing. If anyone is looking at you close enough to notice that you are using a breathing pattern, then they are creepy and you should probably back away slowly.

Don't forget that this takes practice. The only reason that I can give myself a quick shot of relaxation in the middle of a stressful situation is that my body and mind have been trained to do so. You need to practice this often in non-stressful situations. When you are at home by yourself, right before you go to bed, in the car on the way to work… basically whenever you can get it in. My suggestion when starting out is to practice this at least three times per week.

Here's what a typical practice session looks like for me. I lie down on the couch and close my eyes. I let myself breathe normally for a few seconds and just notice the rate that I am naturally breathing. I feel the rise and fall of my chest as start to slow my breathing down. Before jumping into the 4-7-8, I will usually do a few sets of 4-4-4 just to get in the mood. Then I will start my 4-7-8s and do this for as few as 5 minutes or as long as 15 minutes. Try not to stress yourself out about the particulars.

Don't make it an unpleasant experience, because then you will start to resent it. Breathing is your friend. Remember that whole beating your brain into submission thing from before? Well the same thing applies here. Your body is going to resist you at first. You're going to feel like this is the most boring damn thing in the world and that you could really spend your time more effectively. You mind will race and relaxation won't come easily. That's okay. Keep practicing. Once you forge those pathways and develop that muscle memory just like the basketball free throws, it will come so much more easily. This means that when you are first trying to learn a breathing technique, you need to put in a lot of work and practice as often as you can. Once you start to get the hang of it, you can back off a bit and just do some maintenance training every once in a while.

I hope that once you learn this skill, you never have to use it during a panic attack or something. I really do. But if you do find yourself in that situation, believe me when I say that you will be thanking your past self for practicing when you did.

The last thing that I want to mention about breathing is another resource that is available for when you have a few minutes to really focus on your relaxation. There are a lot of great guided relaxations out there that walk you through different steps designed to bring you into a state of calm and relaxation. Guided relaxations (or guided meditations) can come in several forms including text, audio, or video. There are tons of great free ones on youtube or through apps on your phone. Just pop in your headphones, close your eyes for a bit, and bliss out. I'm going to include a script that I wrote for a full body progressive muscle relaxation that you can read. I guarantee that it will make you feel good if you decide to breathe along while you read. I'll put this script into the appendix at the back, though. I take my guided relaxations seriously. I don't swear at you or make bad jokes in the script. We'll keep that gentle stuff separate. Just promise me you'll imagine that my voice sounds like Bob Ross when you read through it.

Ch. 4 Don't be a Jerk to Yourself

Seriously, just don't be. It takes more than the strategies that I've described so far to really kick anxiety in the ass. You need to set yourself up for success too. You need to invest in yourself. You need to stop being a butthead and sabotaging yourself. Let me take a wild guess here. Your life is pretty stressful. Things seem to happen quickly and often times there are factors that are out of your control but that significantly contribute to your level of anxiety. You have this high level of kinetic energy inside of you and sometimes it feels like you can't stop the hamster from running at full speed and it just won't fall off the wheel even though it's so tired that it could die. About 60% of you just nodded your heads, so I feel good about this next part that I'm going to advise you on.

YOU NEED TO TAKE A DAMN BREAK. Actually, you need to take several breaks. Actually, you should take several breaks EVERY DAY. I know. Crazy concept, right? One of the annoying things about anxiety is that it almost never occurs in isolation. If you are the type of person to carry a lot of worry, especially about unfinished business, you are also probably the type to feel really guilty when you do things *other* than those pieces of unfinished business. Guilt is such a shitty thing. As if things weren't hard enough with the anxiety symptoms, guilt just creeps right up in there and makes things exponentially more difficult. I like to call this snowballing. You get worked up and then getting worked up makes you feel bad and then you get more worked up about feeling bad about getting worked up and then.... you get the point.

So yeah, back to the breaks. What if I told you that taking breaks and doing nice things for yourself was not a waste of time? What if I said that they were not counterproductive but actually one of the most productive uses of your time? I... don't have a punchline for that one, but it's the truth. By taking breaks, you are taking the time and investing it in your future self. If you let yourself snowball and reach the point of burnout (a state of pure blah), then any work you do is going to suck anyways. By investing time in yourself, you give yourself a chance to recharge your batteries. I'll talk more about the types of breaks and what you can do to invest in yourself, but the concept is really important. When you relax and recharge, you are gaining strength and clarity. You are enabling yourself to work, make decisions, and just exist more efficiently and effectively in the future.

Well what kind of breaks? That depends. What recharges your batteries? Some people love going out and getting a drink with their friends to relax and recover energy. For those of you are that are introverted in nature, a night out with friends would leave you feeling drained and empty when you get home. Probably not the best choice for your breaks. You gotta do something that fits with you as a person. For me, a big one is playing video games. It seems lazy, but it relaxes me and as long as I put limits on myself, I feel much better and more refreshed afterward. A few of these chapters were cranked out in like 20 minutes right after a League of Legends game.

Another way that you can be nicer to yourself is by replacing some of that asshole language that you use toward yourself in your head. Since I already read my own chapter on cognitions, I know that I can't read your mind, but I can take a pretty educated guess that the things you say to yourself (self-talk) aren't always friendly. Things like, "I'm bad at everything," "I have terrible luck," "that was my fault," or "omg I look so stupid right now." This negative self-talk is something that you probably aren't even aware of, but it eats away at you bit by bit and erodes that self-confidence you need to tackle your anxiety. It's not much use fighting your thoughts. Whatever you do right now... **don't think of a *purple monkey***. I bet you thought of a purple monkey. Fighting against your thoughts is not an effective strategy, so what you can do instead is focus on replacement language. Give yourself some mantras to repeat to yourself throughout the day or when you are actively experiencing symptoms. You can even write them on your bathroom mirror or put them as the wallpaper on your phone. Here's a few you can use:

DBT statements

- I'm allowed to make mistakes
- I'm allowed to feel good sometimes
- Anxiety is my bitch
- I don't like these feelings, but they won't hurt me
- I'm going to be alright

The last thing that I want to mention about taking better care of yourself is some basic stuff. It's basic stuff that you are probably terrible about adhering to, though. This is the part where I tell you that your body is a temple. Well it is! Take care of it. You don't have to do the whole ultra gluten free level 5 vegan juice diet crap, but treat your body well. Don't eat tons of junk food without getting some green in your life every once in a while. Don't drink excessive amounts of alcohol when it's not your birthday. Try to drink more water than you do now, because I'm sure you don't drink enough of it. Sleep is a topic for another book, but resting is really important. Interestingly, sleep is totally vital for learning new skills, which is what I've been bitching at you about this whole time. During sleep, you consolidate new memories, so that you can reach up in there and pull them out when you need to. So get plenty of sleep and keep beating that brain into submission with your new awesome anxiety slaying skills.

Ch. 5 Technology is your Frenemy

The matrix has you. We are all plugged in and as much as we like to think that we use technology as a tool... sometimes it seems that we are the tools and technology is using us. Don't get me wrong, I fucking love technology. If it weren't for google drive, e-readers, text messaging, and internet radio, this project would have never seen the light of day. One thing that I've noticed in my professional training as a therapist is that the older generation of shrinks out there just don't quite get the influence of technology on modern life and modern mental health. I really think that technology has changed the landscape of anxiety. There are many things that it is great for. You can use technology to really facilitate your domination of anxiety, but it can also feed into that anxiety and the bitch about it is that sometimes those two scenarios look almost identical.

This topic is very personally loaded. Not just in my personal experience, but for my wife, who has been gracious enough to allow me to blab about her in this book. She has issues with anxiety. Sometimes it's not so bad and she can go about her day and do important things. Other days, she can get thrown into a panic attack as she's trying to go to sleep and completely unravel within a few minutes. The reason I'm talking about her here is that she is self-employed as a blogger, author, calligrapher, wedding designer etc. Like so many of you out there who are self-employed or just work for modern companies, that means she lives her life on the internet and interfaces with technology for everything.

It's amazing what you can do with the world at your fingertips. Just right now, she was like, "Hey send me a quote from the book to make a graphic out of," and I was all like, "Yo… there's a doc in the drive." Pretty awesome. With the pervasiveness of technology and our lives becoming one with "the cloud" it is sometimes hard to understand where work ends and life begins. When part of your job is keeping up with blogs, does reading them count as a break anymore? Having emails delivered directly to your phone is great, but what about when it is interrupting dinner or stressing you out right before you go to sleep? You gotta get that shit under control before it controls you. Rage against the machine, my friend.

There is no one right answer to the "correct way" to interface with technology, but in general, you just want to set yourself up for success. You want to do a little bit of lifestyle min-maxing. Minimize the ways that technology can intrusively set you off course or influence your mood and maximize the ways it can facilitate your use of anxiety slaying tools.

Here's one. Raise your hand if you use your phone as an alarm in the morning. Ok, now raise your hand if the first thing you do after turning the beeping on your phone off is to open your groggy sleep-filled eyes enough to check your email. That's what I thought. You ever heard of waking up on the wrong side of the bed? Well that's one great way to do it. If you have a stressful email or something that is going to screw up your mood for the day, then you just completely sabotaged yourself. What's the point in doing that, really? Unless you are waiting for an email that contains your schedule for the morning, I'm fairly certain that it can wait until you've taken a shower, gotten dressed, and had your coffee. Remember the whole invest in yourself and recharge your batteries thing? Well you're doing the opposite of that. I dare you to try and remain spritely after waking up to an angry email from a client.

So what can you do about it? This depends a little bit on your job or lifestyle. Definitely do something that fits with your role and the expectations of you. I don't want you blaming me if you get in trouble at work. There are a lot of ways that you can help set yourself up for success in this way, though. Give yourself office hours. Regardless of what your professional or academic life may entail, give yourself personal office hours. Set an auto-responder on your email to anyone that emails you outside of those hours letting them know when you will be able to respond to emails. Simple. If you never stop that flow of information, you're going to start sucking at responding anyways and then no one is happy.

There are a lot of people that I really look up to for their ability to maintain "inbox zero" and avoid killing themselves with email. Tim Ferriss, the author of The Four Hour Workweek, has talked about his technique of checking his email just twice per day. He downloads all of his current emails and then goes offline to a coffee shop or something like that, where he can respond in full to the important emails without the risk of being interrupted by more emails flowing in. This is just one example of one way to manage it, but the point I'm trying to make is that you gotta grab this bull by the horns before one of those horns ends up… somewhere you don't want it to be.

As the chapter name suggests, technology can definitely be a friend as well. I would be nowhere without all of my gadgets and gizmos. With a little creativity, there are some nifty ways that you can make technology work for you and help you manage your anxiety. Here's one that I use. Remember the breaks that I talked about in the previous chapter? Well since you are such a jerk to yourself and it is against your very nature to take the chance to relax and recharge, you can use technology to help you out. Here's a conversation I often have with Siri (the iPhone voice thingy). "Siri, remind me to take a break today." "Okay, Robert. When should I remind you?" "Umm… in an hour." "Alright! Reminder set." Simple as that. When an hour comes around, I will get my reminder to take a break and even though I may not feel entitled to one, I dare not disobey my robot overlord.

There are also tons of great apps and stuff that you can use to streamline your life and facilitate your quest to a better you. I can't mention a ton of specific ones, because they are changing every week, but I would have a look around your phone's app store and see what's available. There are apps that help you with your deep breathing and give you different guided options depending on your current mood. There are also journaling apps to help you just get it all out. There are extensions for Chrome that will let you block websites that stress you out or limit your access to email within certain hours. You can really go crazy with these. Just remember to not go down the rabbit hole of fake productivity and look for new and cool apps for 4 hours right before you go to bed. Don't make the solutions part of the problem.

One good way to understand the ways in which technology might be interfering with your life or disrupting your mood is to track your activities throughout the day. I don't mean tracking the general things you are doing each hour. I mean hardcore, obsessive, annoying tracking of every single thing you do. You really only need to do if for a day, but every time you switch the tab to Facebook, every time you go to that blog of that person you hate, every time you check your work email when you should be enjoying your lunch, you will start to see the effects laid out there for you. It's pretty scary actually. As I said... the matrix has you.

Ch. 6 The Secret

Secret? Oooo mysterious. This isn't like the other secret that you've been told about in other books where you think happy thoughts and then magically good things start happening to you. This is a bit of a side note, but you should really be careful with that sort of thinking. If you get in the habit of thinking that positive thoughts bring about positive things and negative thoughts bring about negative things, it can get really damn confusing when you realize that the universe is random and bad things can happen while you are thinking your happiest magical pixie dust thoughts. ANYWAYS. My secret is that I haven't been entirely honest with you so far. Sorry. The secret is that when I talk about slaying anxiety, kicking it in the balls, or any of the other stupid things that I've said so far, I don't mean that you will be able to make it disappear from your life. Just like you can't make your stupid boss go away forever, you can't make anxiety suddenly poof away in a cloud of smoke. What you are working towards in your recovery from anxiety issues is not only to help yourself avoid unnecessary anxiety when it's possible, but also to learn how to better *tolerate* your anxiety symptoms.

One of the things that really maintains and worsens anxiety symptoms and panic symptoms is the phenomenon of getting worked up about the symptoms themselves. Don't forget, your brain is a douche sometimes and it's very easy to let it tell you that you should be angry, upset, or scared about the fact that you are experiencing anxiety.

Don't get me wrong, anxiety sucks. That's why you got this book. Anxiety is just a thing though. It's a storm that you can weather and come out on the other side. If you are in the ocean surfing and you occasionally get rocked by a wave, it's probably not the best idea to freak out and get super upset. If you did that, you'd thrash around underwater, probably skin your knee on some rock, and then come back up just to get rocked in the face by another wave. A better approach is to endure the wave, stay under the water for a bit until it passes and then try your best to prepare for the next set of waves rolling in.

Anxiety is just like those waves. The better you can learn to tolerate the discomfort of anxiety and recognize it as temporary, the less it will disrupt your life. I'm not trying to tell you to surrender to your anxiety. Not by any means. You're still here to kick this thing's ass, but fighting so hard against the anxiety head-on is not the best strategy because it fights back and then things start to snowball and get blown out of proportion.

A large handful of you probably experience socially related anxiety. The thought of going into a crowded place with tons of noise, no clear path through the mob, and no great means of escape if you get stressed out probably makes you breathe faster and tighten up in the chest without even being in the situation yet. What happens when you can't reason away the feelings that arise? What happens when no matter how hard you breathe, your heart won't go back to its normal resting rate? Nothing. The answer is that nothing happens. You are in the middle of a bunch of people and you have this internal discomfort that probably no one else even notices or cares about. Humans have a tendency to move away and to avoid the situation, but paradoxically, the best option for you is move toward the stressful thing. This is called *exposure.*

You can help temper yourself to better withstand anxiety by allowing yourself to gain exposure to the things that cause you anxiety. For some people, the Kool-Aid man method works the best. This is where you just bust through that wall of anxiety and endure what happens on the other side full force (OHHH YEAHHHHH). For many people, this is a bit too much. That's okay. You don't have to get there all at once. You can break things up into smaller, more manageable increments, and work toward feeling more and more able to withstand the discomfort of anxiety.

Say you want to run a marathon. You aren't necessarily going to go out your first day and run a gazillion miles, expecting to be in shape afterward. No, you start out by just getting off your ass and taking a walk. Then you run around the block. Then you run a mile. Then you run 5 miles. So on and so forth. If you want to feel less anxiety when you give presentations at work, in addition to adjusting your thoughts and being good to your body, you can create a system to systematically desensitize yourself that anxiety. In other words, you keep lifting until you're jacked like Arnold....in an emotional sense.

So, what this might look like is first imagining yourself standing in front of your peers at work. That's it. Just imagining. If the thought of that is enough to cause you anxiety, then you are starting in the right place. So here you are sitting in your yoga pants at home imagining this workplace situation and you start sweating your ass off and hyperventilating. Good. You're at home, nothing bad is going to happen to you. Try some of those deep breathing exercises while you stay in that situation and then just wait it out. I promise you the discomfort won't last forever. Move through, not away. Then you do it again and again until you got that scenario on lock. No problem.

Then it's time to kick it up a notch. Keep imagining that situation and this time actually practicing giving the presentation. Probably a little more stressful? Weather the storm, work through it, then kick it up a notch again. Go to the actual room that you will be giving the presentation in and let that freak you out for a bit. No biggie, though. Weather it, work through it, kick it up a notch. When you get to the day of the presentation, you're going to think, "Shit, shit, shit! That asshole Robert didn't give me a way to practice the actual real thing!" Well you're right and you're wrong. You probably can't practice the actual thing exactly how it will occur in real life, but what you have practiced now is the secret that I have been blabbing about this whole time. You have been practicing feeling anxious and kicking ass anyway.

Ch. 7 The A Team (Anxiety Disorders)

So far I have been fairly non-specific regarding the anxiety symptoms that I have described. That's for good reason. I want you to understand the beast in general before taking a look into its more hardcore forms. In this chapter I am going to describe the anxiety disorders to you. These are psychological disorders that are clinical in nature. I need to stress to you that you *should not* and really *cannot* diagnose yourself. Leave that to the professionals… we need jobs too. I know it's difficult because you are a hypochondriac and can just look up the symptoms, but trust me on this one. You are more than just a checklist. The following disorders are not an exhaustive list, nor are they presented in their pure technical definitions. There are a lot of different criteria for determining these disorders and I really just want you to get the gist of it.

Let's start with **generalized anxiety disorder** (GAD). GAD is really a pain in the ass, because it is pretty hard to pin down. A hallmark feature of GAD is that it is non-specific. Unlike some of the other disorders that I will talk about, there is typically no identifiable stressor that is causing anxiety. Instead you basically have a persistent sense of fear and worry and become overly concerned with everyday matters to the point that the worry interferes with your ability to function well in life. If you have GAD, you will likely have a difficult time making decisions or remembering important things. Think of it this way. Remember how I told you anxiety is like a fire before? Well with GAD you are basically roasting yourself like some low and slow BBQ. Woody Allen is someone that comes to mind as being on the highly neurotic side of this disorder. Everything is a big deal and all big deals lead to stress.

One of the shitty things about GAD is the associated physical symptoms. Panic attacks, which I will talk more about in a sec, are terrible, but they are also awesome in that they usually come and go in a matter of minutes. With GAD you aren't so lucky. You have many of the same features of a panic attack, typically to a lesser degree, but for a really long period of time. Your body isn't designed to be under that sort of stress reaction for those extended periods and so you may find that you constantly have an upset stomach, muscle soreness, difficulty sleeping, constant fatigue etc. It's not fun.

Next up on the A team, we have **panic disorder** (PD). Now this is one that has constantly changing criteria, so I won't get too wildly granular with this description. The general idea has to do with those panic attacks that we talked about earlier in the "Your Body is an Asshole too" chapter. Basically, when you have PD, you experience those panic attacks where you have strong physical symptoms combined with intense fear and discomfort. They tend to peak at around 10 minutes and then cool down. The party isn't over after that, though. The defining feature of PD is that after you have a panic attack, you suffer from intense fear of having another one.

PD really sucks because you can start to have anxiety symptoms outside of legit panic attacks because you are so afraid of having another one and not being able to cope. It's really a lose lose situation, because being so preoccupied about the potential of future attacks makes you more sensitized and vulnerable to them occurring. If you fear them, they shall come.

You are probably familiar with **phobias**. They are pretty straight forward, but people misuse the term quite a bit. To have a phobia does not mean that you dislike something strongly. For a specific phobia, it means that when you are in the presence of the feared object, animal, location etc., you experience intense fear and apprehension. I don't mean you get uncomfortable. I mean you freak the hell out. Another feature of phobias is that you know you are crazy. You know that the amount of fear and discomfort you feel about this thing is in no way proportional to the actual situation.

There are different subtypes of phobias. For instance, there is blood and injection phobia, where you pass out every time you visit the Red Cross. There is also social phobia, which is essentially an intense fear of social situations in which you feel like you have to be on stage and be judged by everyone else even though no one really cares wtf you're doing. This is sometimes classified as a disorder in its own right (social anxiety disorder), but the main bad stuff that you are going to feel is a sense of overwhelming embarrassment or humiliation in most or all social situations.

Next up is **obsessive compulsive disorder** (OCD). I'm just going to throw this out there. The world has no idea what OCD is. Most of what you see on TV or hear people say ("oh that's just my OCD") is referring to OCPD, or obsessive compulsive personality disorder. Basically people who are so anal and finicky that it's super annoying. OCD is a bit more serious.

As you might guess, the two major components of OCD are obsessions and compulsions. Obsessions are disruptive thoughts or images that pop into your head and persist there. These can get really disturbing like imagining yourself crushing kittens or people you love dying. They are repetitive in nature and generally cause serious psychological discomfort. Compulsions are what you might be more familiar with. They are urges to perform very specific or ritualistic acts. A classic example is stepping on every crack (or every 3rd crack) on the sidewalk. These are often linked to the obsessions in a causal way, even though no real cause and effect relationship exists between them. In the previous example, a person with OCD might feel that they MUST step on each crack in the sidewalk otherwise a plane will fall out of the sky and kill everyone inside. Someone else might have to step back and forth 10 times before entering or leaving a house otherwise the home will get robbed. OCD can also exist with only obsessions or only compulsions, but these forms are much less common.

The last anxiety disorder that I'm going to talk about is called **post traumatic stress disorder** (PTSD). You have probably heard of this one in regards to the military. Troops in the armed forces are one of the most likely populations to get PTSD and it's a huge problem in the United States right now. Basically PTSD is when you experience or witness some really fucked up stuff and it messes up your head.

The traumatic event doesn't have to be just combat but it can also include things like natural disasters, physical abuse, or rape. The group of symptoms that come along with PTSD is pretty distinct. If you know someone who has PTSD, you will know exactly what I'm talking about. The person with PTSD is likely going to have some sort of re-experiencing of the traumatic event either in the form of flashbacks or dreams. They deserve to forget, but their douchebrain keeps going, "Nope! Time to live it all over again." They are also likely to be on edge and hypervigilant. This means that they are always looking for signs of danger and startle a lot more easily than other people. Emotional symptoms are also common with PTSD. These are a little different from person to person. Some become very withdrawn and anti-social, while others explode outward in anger and rage. I fucking hate PTSD. If you did your time and had to live through something so terrible, your brain really should do you a solid and just let you move on. Sigh…

So those are the main villains in our anxiety story. They all deserve to die. Luckily for you, they are most certainly manageable. Many people have had success on their own, with therapy, with medication, or some combination thereof and have been able to change their lives and conquer their anxiety disorders. Don't give up hope if you fit the profile for one of these. Your journey starts now.

Ch. 8 How to Talk to People Who Don't Get It

Okay, so this is cool and futuristic. I tweeted out (@duffthepsych) that I was working on a second edition of this book and asked if anyone had suggestions. One awesome fan made the perfect suggestion of writing a chapter about dealing with people who don't understand anxiety. I can't believe that I didn't initially realize how useful that would be. Well that's exactly what I want to do this chapter because I'm fairly certain that nearly every single person that I have met who suffers from anxiety also suffers from some dumb dumb in their life who just does not get it. Maybe you have heard a few of these gems: "It's all in your head!" "You just need to stop worrying so much!" "Dude, just breathe…" or even "What's your problem?" I'm sure statements like these really help out, right? Of course not.

These are telltale signs that someone simply does not understand what you are going through. Be happy for them. That means that they have not felt the true shittiness of anxiety the way that you have. I do understand that this can be incredibly frustrating though. If this person is family, it tends to amp up the frustration factor even more. I think that often times we try to communicate what it's like to have anxiety and then give up when it doesn't seem to sink in for the other person. The process of trying to communicate clearly and find the right words to say can be anxiety provoking in and of itself. Couple that with the fact that you are exhausted from fighting your own private battle with anxiety all day and it can feel pretty pointless.

I want to help you out by providing some ideas about ways in which you can communicate to these people. Here's what we will do. I will write out a letter of sorts that you could recite out loud or even give as a written/typed note to the person in question. This does not need to be an exact script, but it might get you started in the right direction. After I finish writing the letter, I will retrospectively break down some of the things that I wrote by instinct and try to understand what some of the magic ingredients are for communicating with people who do not understand your anxiety.

To whom this may concern,

You are an important person in this individual's life. That's why you are getting this letter. My name is Robert. I am a therapist and the author of a book about anxiety that this person has recently read. This means that they are trying to find resources to help pull themselves out of the crappy feelings that you have seen them struggling with. It can be immensely hard to explain what anxiety feels like. If you have never had significant issues with anxiety, you are exceptionally lucky because it really sucks. I want you to know that the person who gave you this letter is not trying to be difficult. If they had a magic wand that could help them suddenly stop struggling with these issues, I 100% guarantee that they would use it without a moment's hesitation.

Have you ever felt the "fight or flight" response? Maybe you've stepped out into the street without looking both ways and nearly missed getting hit by a car or perhaps you've had to speak in front of 1000 people and felt like you were going to puke, cry, and hyperventilate all at the same time. That's what anxiety feels like except it's not just a fleeting state of discomfort that happens once. It is something that can come on without much warning and it makes it very difficult to function. Trust me when I say that this person feels sad, guilty, and exhausted due to difficulties that anxiety causes them and the people around them. You don't need to know how to make them feel better and that's okay because it's not your responsibility.

If you want to be awesome, I have a few tips that can help you be the best support possible for this person when they are enduring a hard time. Firstly, don't take it personally. They might act very differently when they are having a "peak" in their anxiety. Take the things that they say and do in context. I'm sure you've been through a hard time before and acted in ways that aren't quite in line with your normal self. Asking them if there is anything that you can do to help is great, but don't always expect to get a clear response from them. Things can be confusing when the anxiety monster is hitting hard, so knowing what would help is not always clear. One question that most anxious people can give you an answer to is "do you need some space?" If they say yes, please give them a little room to breathe and let them know that you will be around if they need you. Try not to tell them it's all in their head, because they know that already. It doesn't make the pounding in their chest, the pain in their head, the hyperventilation, the sweating, or the racing thoughts any easier to deal with. There's no way that I can put you in their shoes, but I hope you believe me when I say that it's not as easy as just taking a breath and getting some fresh air.

Having anxiety does not mean that this person gets a blank slate to do or say anything that they want. You still have a right to be upset if they do shitty things but like I said before, try to take it in context. If you want to address the way that they are acting or the things that they are saying, maybe consider doing it when things have calmed down a bit. I also want make it clear that you don't have to understand them or agree with everything that they do to be supportive. This person's world feels chaotic and a good portion of their unease probably comes from feeling like they have no control over their environment and the things that happen to them. If they know that you are a constant that will be supportive no matter what happens, it can make a big difference.

Lastly, I'd like to tell you good job! If you are still in this person's life, then you aren't like the others who have run away or disappeared on them so far. They need supports on this journey and they really want you to be on their team. If you want to learn more about what this individual's experience with anxiety is like then I encourage you to ask them. I'm sure that when things are at their least crazy, they would be more than happy to sit with you and help you understand.

Sincerely,

Robert Duff, Ph.D. on behalf of the awesome anxiety warrior that gave you this note.

Okay, so that was written basically off the top of my head based on my personal and clinical intuition. Let's break it down a little bit to see what some of the key ingredients are and how you might be able to utilize them to better communicate with these people in your life who are having a hard time understanding your struggle.

The first thing that comes to mind is that these people aren't trying to be annoying or mean when they suggest things to you. These are unsuccessful attempts at solving your problem. You aren't the only one who wants to make this crap go away for you. If they had a magic wand to make you feel better, they would also wave the hell out of it. However, anxiety is something that humans don't come into this world well equipped to handle. What results is someone who cares that you feel better, is frustrated that things have to be this way right now, and has few good tools to do anything about it. Therefore, they tend to go to the things that work for them as a "normie" (someone who doesn't experience these issues). Things like getting some fresh air, distracting yourself with other tasks, or thinking positively may be perfectly acceptable to solutions to a small ounce of everyday stress, but they are barely a starting point for legit anxiety issues. If you would like to communicate this to them, I would say that it can be helpful to do so during a time when you aren't already super anxious. For instance, if you had a blow up the night before and got into a fight over this person ineffectively trying to help you, you might come to them the next day and say something like, "Hey, I'm sorry about yelling at you last night. It's just that it's really hard to deal with in the moment and when you say things like 'just breathe' it can be frustrating because I wish it was that simple. I'm trying to get better and I appreciate you trying to help, but next time I'm so worked up it would help me more if you tried to give me some space and didn't try to suggest so many ways to help."

Another thing that can really help people "get it" is to help them relate your experience to something that they have been through at some point in their life. Things like weddings, exams, job interviews, sports games, emergency situations, and other high stress events are things that you might be able to point to as times that they have felt anxiety. They might say that these are times that everyone feels stressed out, but what they don't understand is that this is pretty much the norm for you. You can say something like, "I want to tell you what it feels like to have this kind of anxiety. When you got married, did you feel nervous? Like right before you walked out and everyone was looking straight at you? Okay, well imagine that being your 'normal' feeling and when actual stress happens, it multiplies and makes you feel terrible."

I think that people also tend to not understand the other component of anxiety, which is the thoughts. Since your thoughts are invisible and you may or may not be making them known verbally, people in your life are likely to not understand what it's like to have a whirlwind inside of your brain of persistent worries about god knows what. A good way to help them understand might be to make the analogy of rumination and worry being like a song that gets stuck in your head. Most people have had a song stuck in their head at some point in time. It's funny at first, then after a while it gets a bit annoying. If it goes on for too long it starts to be downright unpleasant. I'm not talking about your favorite song here. I'm talking about when you get some stupid commercial jingle stuck in your head and you only know one line from the whole song and no matter what you do you can't get it out and you are thinking about getting a spoon and carving the goddamn song straight out of your brain!! Okay that was a bit dramatic, but I think most people will understand what I'm getting at. Now if you can get that person to imagine that intensity of thought and couple it with negative thoughts and worry, they might be able to comprehend just a little more how messed up the experience of anxiety can be.

So that's it for my bonus chapter about ways that you might be able to better talk to those who just don't understand your anxiety. I will go ahead and put a printable of that letter up on my website at **duffthepsych.com/letter** so that you can actually hand it to someone in your life if you think that it will help. Just like everything else in this book, the information and tips contained in this chapter will not fix the entire situation for you, but I hope that these were some different and interesting ways of approaching the task of trying to explain your experience to someone who has never been there.

Ch. 9 Get Your Head Shrunk

I'm not sure why you picked up this book. I am so thankful that you did and I owe you a mega sized hug for it, but I don't know your particular reasons. However, I do bet that there are quite a few of you out there who bought this book because you wanted to see what you could figure out on your own without the help of the therapist. Well good on you. You're a badass and I hope that this totally works out for you. I want to at least mention psychotherapy, though. After all, it is my full-time real person job. People have a lot of different expectations and impressions of therapy, so I want to just talk a bit about what it looks like and how it can help you.

First of all. Therapy is not a club. You don't have to be an A-lister with co-existing OCD and PTSD to get in. Therapy is for everyone. There are also different types of therapy. The most common model in the United States is talk therapy. Depending on who you see, this could be as frequent as once per week or as infrequent as a monthly check-in.

Therapists vary quite a bit in their approaches as well. A more behaviorally oriented therapist will look into the circumstances surrounding your anxiety. What situation provokes the symptoms and where did you first learn to respond that way? They will then work to help you "unlearn" those responses. A cognitively oriented therapist will really dig deep into your thought patterns (we did a little of this earlier). You will be collaborative scientists together and test your thoughts to get to the bottom of whether it makes any sense for you to feel this way. Psychodynamic or insight oriented therapists will take things a bit further and look deep for the origins of your anxiety. They will view anxiety as a symptoms of some deeper underlying issues and work to help you achieve insight into how those issues are playing out in your life.

That is a small sampling of the different types of therapeutic approaches that are utilized currently in the field. There are many more. The other thing to consider is that not all therapists are created equal. I mean it when I say that there are some shrinks that really just suck at their job. It's okay, we are people too. Some people are not good at their job. Maybe they are burnt out from years of clinical work and they know it or maybe they think they are the best ever and can't see that they are just too awkward to ever help you open up. Don't feel bad if you have a bad experience with therapy. You are allowed to shop around. Don't forget that you are a consumer. No one wants you to be wasting time and money on something that isn't going to work for you.

Don't let a single awkward or negative experience prevent you from trying other therapy in the future. The first time I tried Thai food, I thought I hated it. I thought that it was just something that other people could like but it wasn't for me. I realized later on after shopping around a bit and sampling some other restaurants that it was just a bad chef that gave me that impression. Thai food kicks ass. So hungry right now.

The length of treatment can vary quite a bit. Some issues can be resolved in just a few weeks and others might take a lifetime to unearth. In my opinion, a good shrink will start with the immediate stuff, help you find some solid ground to put under your feet, and then when you are a bit more stable, they will work to dig a little deeper to find out where all of this shit really came from. You might also engage in different forms of treatment like group therapy. Groups can be a lot of fun. Typically they involve some educational component where someone much more eloquent but probably less funny than me will explain the topic of the day such as "managing worries" or "how to know when you are panicking," and then the group will discuss together about the topic. Groups are made up of people. Some people are awesome and some people suck. The quality of the group depends on the quality of the people. Again, don't be afraid to shop around.

How do you shop around for therapists? Well it depends on your particular situation. If you are a college student at a university, chances are you're already hooked up with free access to psychotherapy with students in the training program at your school. Don't worry, they won't make things awkward if you see them elsewhere on campus. There are a lot of really strict rules in place about confidentiality. If they were to not respect your privacy, they'd basically be screwed anyways. I worked as a therapist during my doctoral training and some of my regular clients were able to make serious changes in their life. It feels pretty damn great. Often times at these "training clinics" you don't have to be a student to get services, but you would just end up paying for sessions at a much lower rate than you are likely to find out in the community. If you don't have insurance, start there.

Do you have mental health coverage? If so, groovy. These days, you can often go to the insurance provider's website and use their own search engine to find covered providers near you. If they don't have one, you can just use something like Psychology Today's "Find a Therapist" tool and look for therapists that accept your insurance. The neat thing about searching for a therapist online is that you can filter by specialty or type of therapy. You can also check to see if they have their own website, which for someone like me speaks to the character of the therapist.

Don't have insurance? It sucks, I know... been there. There are still options. Look up therapists that have what's called a "sliding scale." This means that the therapist will charge a rate that is consistent with the client's income. If have no income, you could be looking at mega cheap, or in some cases, free sessions. You typically have to provide some sort of proof of income (or lack thereof) so that they know you aren't just trying to work the system. Don't let the discounted price scare you. It doesn't mean that you are going to get budget quality therapy... it just means that some people are awesome and legitimately want to help you. Finally, if you are strapped for cash and without insurance you could also look into community resources. Many counties have non-profit organizations that offer free services to those who are really in need. I should reiterate that my experience is in the United States. I'm not entirely sure how similar therapy and mental health services are in other countries.

I'm going to cut the funny shit for a second here. If you are in need of help that is probably above and beyond what you can do on your own right now, please seek professional help. Family and friends are great, but there will always be a limit to what they can help you out with. From me to you, there is absolutely nothing to be ashamed about. We all fall down sometimes and we are all allowed to have periods of recovery. The help is out there and if you aren't able to find the strength to do this for yourself, that's okay too. Let someone who loves you know and they will be able to help you out. It's not worth it to keep suffering, friend. Let's get you better.

The last thing that I want to mention in this chapter is medication. Now this is something that I initially left out of the first edition of this book. I did that because I wanted to cover my own ass. My role is as a therapist and while I have a doctorate in psychology, I am not a medical doctor and it is beyond my scope to advise you on which medications to take. Many of you wanted to hear more about medication, though, so I am going to give you some of my thoughts about it. At the time of writing this, I am currently working at a large healthcare organization as a therapist. At the end of every intake session with a new patient, I ask them how they would like to follow up. The main buffet of options includes psychotherapy, educational or support groups, and consultation with a psychiatrist to talk about medication. People fall on many different sides of the fence when it comes to medicine. There are a lot of misconceptions out there about medication. People think about movies that they have seen where it zombifies you and makes you unable to feel. There are certainly some medications that have a bit of a sedating effect, but in general this is not what happens. They also aren't a miracle drug. Many medications take a few weeks to alter your brain chemistry and begin working their magic. Some medications are for emergencies only such as when you are actively panicking. As for which are right for you, that is definitely something that you should talk to a psychiatrist about. Psychiatrists are medical doctors that specialize in psychiatric medication. Your primary care can certainly write you a prescription for some anti-anxiety medication, but these particular types of medications can be a bit tricky to dial in. If you have access to a psychiatrist, I would definitely suggest talking to one.

My opinion about medication is that it doesn't solve any problems for you. A pill will not make the issues that create anxiety for you disappear. That said, I think that medication can be invaluable in its ability to help you cope with the crushing pressure of anxiety that sometimes makes it so damn difficult to find those solutions on your own. Basically, the long term medications (non-emergency) help to bring your baseline level of anxiety and reactivity down to a point that you can focus on learning good coping skills in therapy or through your own problem solving. On that note, I also want to say that I definitely suggest taking advantage of both therapy and psychopharmaceutical (drug) treatment if you decide to try out medication. With few exceptions nobody wants you to be on medication for anxiety for the rest of your life. The point is to help raise you up while you build your own emotional scaffolding underneath. That way, if at some point, you feel like you have made progress and want to try this shit out on your own, that scaffolding that you built in the form of skills, knowledge, and perspective will hold you up when that medication support is taken out from underneath you.

Ch. 10 Get Pumped. Do Work.

This chapter doesn't have a particular therapeutic basis or massive research backing it up. This is the freestyle section where I get to geek out and tell you how freaking amped I am for you to get out there and do this damn thing. No, seriously. I wish you could see how fast my fingers are typing right now. You are all coming from different backgrounds with different attitudes and different levels of readiness for change. When you picked up this book, you might already have been amped like me. Maybe you were curious but skeptical. Maybe you were doubtful but thought you'd give at least one more shot at feeling better. In all of those situations, you still picked up the damn book. You're ready for this.

You are in a period of progress. Whether it's a little tweaking that you want to do or a radical overhaul, allow this period of your life to be one that you work on yourself. There's no timeline on healing, but there's also no time like the present to start making some changes. The anxious brain is likely to take that statement and feel like that is a lot of pressure. You might think, "Do I HAVE to get better now?" or, "Should I be better by now?" No way! It's all good. These things can take time, but you're already closer to the version of you that you want to be than you were before you read this book. In fact, if the prospect of changing everything all at once is daunting or scary to you, then break it up into smaller pieces.

Get out a sheet of paper and write down the things that stuck with you from this book. Write down the things that you don't have to go back and re-read to remember. Even if you can't remember the full details, write down a few general concepts. Now think about the aspects of your anxiety that are causing you the most grief. Which pieces are really screwing with you? Boom. You just found a place to start.

Is there one of those issues that seems to line up well with the concepts you learned in this book? You bet your ass there is! Set yourself up with a plan for success. What is one small thing that you can do to get started on your quest? Maybe it's forcing yourself to take 3 short breaks during your week to reinvest your energy. Maybe you want to start keeping a little notebook with you to use as a thought log through your day. Maybe you even want to finally use that gym membership you've had for half a year and listen to that catchy ass new T-Swift song on the elliptical.

The point I'm trying to make is that you can start now and be super stoked about taking these first steps toward really creating some enduring change in your life. You may even find that you have now given yourself permission to change and you will begin to naturally improve on your own. I promise you that there will be days that you feel crazy motivated and resilient and others where you feel like you are losing the uphill battle. These are normal things. The graph of improvement over time is never a perfect line. There will be ups and downs, but you *will* be trending upward. My best advice to you is to try to be enthusiastic about this in a way that makes sense to you.

I'll tell you how I stay motivated. I named my anxiety. No seriously. His name is Fred and he's a fucking pain in the ass. I hate him. He's annoying, mean, pushy, rude, and he constantly smells like cabbage. Now, I'm not one for real interpersonal violence (unless it's in the octagon), but when I wake up and I'm in one of my periods of progress, I say to myself, "You're goin' down, Fred." I also love video games, so I make a game out of it. Exposure is like gaining experience leveling up my character. Getting better at deep breathing is like improving my fireball skill. Learning a new coping skill is like stumbling upon some epic imbued weapon. You should see my character at this point... much more badass than my actual outward appearance.

There are a zillion ways to get the work done. Maybe for you, you can conceptualize it as building yourself this swaggarific castle. Sometimes you have to first build the foundation and some scaffolding, then you can hire more hands, upgrade your tools, and eventually build the crap out of that thing. From then on, it's just occasional maintenance from stray catapult shots or dragon fire throughout the years.

Find something that works for you. This is your deal. You can go it alone or bring some friends along for the ride. You can pack it all in at once or take it slow and gradual. Whatever the case may be, you are ready to get started now. I'm getting chills thinking about how fucking awesome you are. Get pumped, my friend. Do work.

Thank You

You did not have to purchase this book, but you did. For that I thank you. If you enjoyed what you read, please consider leaving an honest review on Amazon. This will help the book reach a broader audience. If you have particular feedback about the book that you would like to share, please email duffthepsych@gmail.com with the subject "feedback".

It was my absolute pleasure to write this book and I am more than a little excited to continue the series. I encourage you to continue to keep up with the series by joining the Email list at hardcoreselfhelp.com, following on twitter @duffthepsych, or liking the Duff the Psych Facebook page.

-Robert

Appendix

Guided Muscle Relaxation - Approximately 10 minutes

Guided Muscle Relaxation - Approximately 10 minutes

Before you begin this exercise, get into a comfortable position. You can sit or lie down. Bring your hands to rest by your sides or in your lap. In this guided relaxation, I will be asking you to tense various muscle groups in your body and then release the tension. If you have injuries or pain that would make any part of this uncomfortable, feel free to skip over them. If you would like a longer experience, simply tense each muscle group two times for a more complete relaxation.

Take a moment to notice your breathing. Feel the rise and fall of your chest. You have a unique rhythm to your breath that belongs to you alone. Take some time to just be mindful and appreciative of this rhythm. Take in the awareness of how your body feels as it is supported by the furniture that you rest on. In your mind, scan your body from bottom to top and notice any areas of tension or pain.

You are first going to relax your feet. Take a deep breath in and as you do, curl your toes downward to tense up the muscles in your feet. Hold that tension for a moment and then exhale, releasing both your breath and the tension in your feet. Allow your foot to fall limp and relaxed.

Next, you will focus on the calf muscles in your lower legs. You can tense these muscles by pointing your toes downward. Do this now while breathing in a deep cleansing breath. Hold the tension. Now release. Exhale and allow your calf muscles to relax completely.

Move to the muscles in your upper legs now. You put much strain on this part of your body from walking around all day and when you exercise. You can tense these muscles by pushing your feet into the ground while sitting or by stretching your legs out straight while lying down. Take a nice deep breath and tense the muscles in your thighs. Hold it for just a moment and then release everything. Notice the flow of blood into your muscles, which are now more soft and relaxed. It might feel tingly and warm. Enjoy this feeling for a moment before moving on.

Now you will tighten your glute muscles on your back side. These take much abuse from sitting for long periods. Take in a deep breath and clench these muscles tightly. You should feel your body rise a little. Keep that tension for as long as you are comfortable and then release it as you exhale away your stress and worry.

Take in another slow breath and tense all of the muscles in your legs. Do this in any way that feels natural and comfortable for you. Hold it… now release all of these strong muscles and let the tensions melt away with your outbreath. Notice that you are feeling more and more deeply relaxed.

Now, bring your awareness to your stomach. Draw in a long breath and tense your abdominal muscles in a way that feels comfortable for you. Keep that tension for a moment and then release it as you exhale.

Next, you are going to focus on the muscles in your back. Draw in a nice deep breath and as you do, arch your back slightly and tighten the muscles there. Hold for just a moment and then release as you slowly return to your original position.

Move up to the muscles in your shoulders. Often it feels as though we carry a great weight in our shoulders. Take care of them now by breathing in deeply and pulling your shoulders up toward your ears. Keep this tensions in your shoulders and neck for a few seconds and then slowly return to your previous position while exhaling. Allow the tension to be carried away with your breath.

Feel the heaviness in your body now. You should feel as though the furniture you are on is supporting you more fully than when you began. Your muscles are increasingly becoming soft and relaxed.

Now it's time to let go of the tension in your arms and your hands. You can tighten your forearms by raising your wrists and bending your hands backward toward your body. Take a deep breath and tense your forearm muscles in this way. Hold it for a few moments and then exhale fully as you let go of that tension.

Next, take a long breath and curl your wrists up toward your shoulders to tense up the muscles in your upper arm. Hold this for as long as you feel comfortable and then release your breath as you slowly lower your arms.

Your hands also deserve attention. As you breathe in, clench your fists tightly. Hold this tension to the best of your ability. Exhale and slowly open your hands. Take a moment to allow the blood to flow back into your fingers and enjoy the sensation as they become limp and relaxed.

You are nearing a state of complete relaxation.

Now tighten the muscles in your face by squeezing your eyes shut and clenching your lips together. As you do, breathe in full and hold it. Now breathe out and relax all of the muscles in your face. Allow your facial expression to become soft and effortless.

You are now relaxed from the tips of your toes to the top of your head. Take a few more nice deep breaths and imagine them cleansing your entire body. You are free from stress. You are calm. You are safe.

Please take as much time as you would like to enjoy this relaxation. When you are ready, you can open your eyes and return to your day or you may fall asleep.

Informal References by Chapter

Intro:
- I probably made these books up. Any real titles are purely coincidental.
- "Moral of the Story" from the album Cardboard Castles by Watsky, 2013.

Ch 1:
- I'm aware that I mixed my comic book universes. Hulk is Marvel and Flash is DC. Deal with it.
- Key players in cognitive behavioral therapy include Albert Ellis and Aaron Beck.

Ch 3:
- Bob Ross should need no introduction, but you can learn a lot from his theory on happy accidents.

Ch 4:
- Level 5 Vegan: someone who doesn't eat anything with a shadow. From an episode of The Simpsons.

Ch 5:
- The Matrix is a great movie. Maybe not the whole trilogy, but dat Matrix tho.
- Drive and Chrome both by Google. Thanks Google!
- Siri is the voice recognition robot concierge by Apple.
- Four Hour Work Week is a book by Tim Ferriss that teaches you how to work more efficiently, so that you can spend more time doing the things that you love with the people that you love.

Ch 6:
- The Secret by Rhonda Byrne, 2006.
- The Kool-Aide guy makes a great cameo in Family Guy

Ch 7:

- The Diagnostic and Statistical Manual (DSM) is the handbook that psychologists use to diagnose mental disorders. Don't diagnose yourself.

Ch 10:

- At the time of writing, Taylor Swift just put out her new single "Shake It Off" and it's way too damn catchy.
- The octagon is the arena of combat for the mixed martial arts organization UFC.
- I lost many years of my life to Diablo II. I regret nothing.

Made in the USA
San Bernardino, CA
17 December 2015